The Crane-Riding Immortal
騎鶴的仙人

有一句話說：「狗咬呂洞賓，不識好人心。」小朋友，你知道呂洞賓是誰嗎？原來呂洞賓就是八仙裏頭的一位神仙。

傳說呂洞賓的母親快要生下他的時候，有一隻仙鶴從天上衝下來，飛入帳裏就不見了。

大家都說，這孩子一定不是平凡的人。果然呂洞賓生下以後就有一副仙人的模樣。

There is a children's rhyme that goes, "Like a dog biting Lyu Dungbin, you are blind to a person's goodness." Children, do you know who is Lyu Dungbin? Well, he is one of the Eight Immortals.

Legend says that when Lyu Dungbin's mother was about to give birth to him, an angelic crane rushed from heaven and disappeared under the canopy where Lyu's mother was resting.

Everyone said that her child would grow up to be an extraordinary man. In fact, from birth Lyu Dungbin was gifted with the build of an immortal.

Lyu Dungbin's portrait

3

呂洞賓從小就很聰明，每天能夠背很多文章，可惜他的運氣不好，考了兩次試都沒考上。

他六十四歲那年，在酒樓遇見一位神仙。神仙看他相貌不平常，就問他有什麼志向。呂洞賓說他很想修道做神仙，神仙很高興，就帶著他上山修道去了！

Even as a little child, Lyu Dungbin was very smart. Every day, he would memorize many essays. Unfortunately, he did not have any luck in passing the civil examination for government positions. Twice he tried, and twice he failed.

When he was sixty-four years old, he met an immortal in a tavern. The immortal recognized Lyu Dungbin's striking facial features, and immediately asked Lyu of his goals in life. Lyu Dungbin said that he really wanted to discipline himself to become an immortal as well. Lyu's reply pleased the immortal. Consequently, he invited Lyu to the mountains for training.

　　呂洞賓苦修了十幾
年的道，又通過神仙一
關、一關的考試，終於
得道成仙了。
　　呂洞賓雖然成了仙
人，可以到天上去，但
是，他看到民間百姓還
有很多苦難，所以決心
留在民間，幫助天下有
困苦的百姓。

Lyu Dungbin diligently studied with the immortal for some ten years, passing examinations, one after the other. Finally, he acquired the skills of an immortal.

Even though Lyu Dungbin had now become an immortal and could go to heaven, he decided to stay among the common folk to help ease their suffering.

有一天，呂洞賓來到一家酒樓。他想試試酒樓老闆是不是心地善良，就裝成窮人，吃完酒菜，沒付錢就走了！第二天，呂洞賓又來了，老闆也沒向他要錢。呂洞賓仍然吃喝一頓，拍拍屁股又走了。就這樣白吃白喝了半年，酒樓老闆都不介意。

呂洞賓終於相信這老闆心地很好，於是對他說：「我欠了你不少酒錢，我看這樣吧！我畫一隻鶴在你的牆上，以後有客人來，就喊鶴下來跳舞，相信可以替你招來不少生意，你多賺的錢，就算是我付你的酒錢吧！」說完，在牆上畫了一隻黃鶴，然後就走了。

One day, Lyu Dungbin arrived at a tavern. He wanted to test the owner to see if he was good at heart. So, he pretended to be a poor man. After he ate and drank, he left without paying a cent! The next day, Lyu Dungbin went to the tavern again, and the owner did not ask him for any money either. Lyu Dungbin had another round of drinking and eating, and again, he left without a sense of guilt. So, for half a year, Lyu ate and drank freely, and the tavern owner did not mind it a bit.

Lyu Dungbin was finally convinced of the tavern owner's virtue and said to him, "I owe you very much money. Let me repay you this way. I'll draw a crane on your wall. Then you'll be able to call it down to dance whenever you have customers. I'm sure it'll bring good luck to your business. So, let the extra money you earn be my payment to you." After he finished talking, Lyu drew a yellow crane on the wall and left immediately.

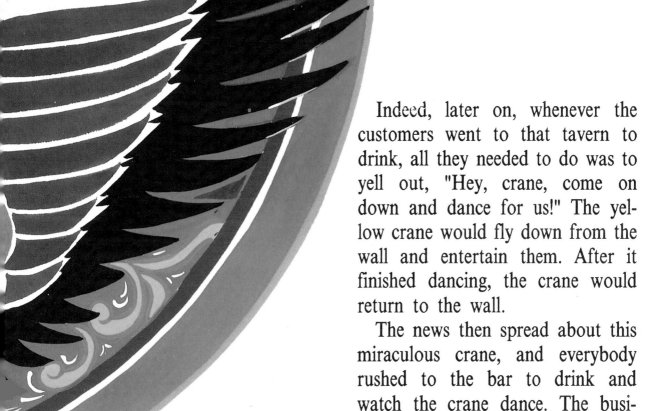

Indeed, later on, whenever the customers went to that tavern to drink, all they needed to do was to yell out, "Hey, crane, come on down and dance for us!" The yellow crane would fly down from the wall and entertain them. After it finished dancing, the crane would return to the wall.

The news then spread about this miraculous crane, and everybody rushed to the bar to drink and watch the crane dance. The business got better and better each day. After a few years, the tavern owner became a very rich man.

果然，以後客人到酒樓喝酒，只要喊一聲：「鶴呀！下來跳個舞吧！」黃鶴就會從牆上飛下來跳舞，跳完又飛回牆上。

這件神奇的事傳開以後，大家都爭著到酒樓喝酒、看鶴跳舞。酒樓的生意一天比一天好，幾年以後，酒樓老闆就成了大富翁了。

Later Lyu Dungbin went back to the tavern. The owner cheerfully said to him, "Thank you very much for drawing me that crane. Now I have become rich!" Lyu Dungbin replied with a laugh, "Then, my bill is settled!" After he finished speaking, he clapped his hands, and the yellow crane flew down from the wall. Lyu Dungbin climbed onto the crane and flew away!

Only then did the tavern owner realize that the artist was actually an immortal. Later, the owner renovated the tavern and named it the "Yellow Crane Pavilion."

有一天呂洞賓忽然又回到酒樓，酒樓老闆高興的對他說：「多謝您替我畫了一隻鶴，現在我發財了！」呂洞賓笑著說：「那我就不欠你了！」說完，他兩手一拍，只見黃鶴飛了下來，呂洞賓就騎著鶴飛走了！

酒樓老闆這才知道，這畫鶴的是個神仙。於是他把酒樓重新整修，取名爲「黃鶴樓」。

Nowadays, the "Yellow Crane Pavilion" is known as a famous historical site in Hubei Province. Many tourists visiting the "Yellow Crane Pavilion" often hear about Lyu Dungbin riding the crane.

現在黃鶴樓已經成了湖北省的名勝古蹟，許多遊客到黃鶴樓去玩，還常常談起呂洞賓騎鶴的事呢！

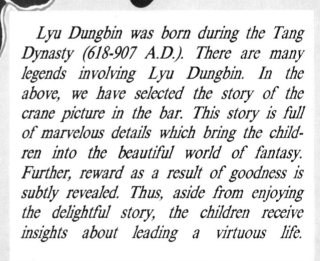

Parental Guide

Lyu Dungbin was born during the Tang Dynasty (618-907 A.D.). There are many legends involving Lyu Dungbin. In the above, we have selected the story of the crane picture in the bar. This story is full of marvelous details which bring the children into the beautiful world of fantasy. Further, reward as a result of goodness is subtly revealed. Thus, aside from enjoying the delightful story, the children receive insights about leading a virtuous life.

Lyu Dungbin & Guanyin

呂洞賓追觀音

　　小朋友，上一篇我們講了呂洞賓騎鶴的故事，現在，我們要講的是呂洞賓有趣的戀愛故事。

　　傳說呂洞賓長得非常英俊瀟灑，個兒高高的，身材十分雄偉。說到面貌嘛，他有一雙丹鳳眼，兩道長眉毛，再加上挺直的鼻子，真可說是一個美男子哩！

　　呂洞賓因為自己長得很英俊，所以認為只有漂亮女孩才配得上他，於是他東挑西選，最後覺得觀音娘娘最美麗，便想追求觀音娘娘，打算娶她當妻子。

Children, in the last chapter, we have talked about the story of Lyu Dungbin riding the crane. Now, we will talk about the Lyu Dungbin's interesting love story .

Legend says that Lyu Dungbin was very handsome. He was quite tall with an impressive build. In terms of his facial features, he had eyes like that of a red phoenix and a pair of long eyebrows; considering this and his upright nose, he was really a handsome man!

Since Lyu Dungbin also knew that he was very handsome, he thought that only a beautiful woman could be his companion. Hence, he would pick and choose among the most beautiful. In the end, he felt that Lady Guanyin, the Goddess of Mercy, was the most beautiful of all. She would be the one that he would court and marry.

One day, Lyu Dungbin went to visit Lady Guanyin. He brought her a gift and asked her to marry him. However, Lady Guanyin had begun learning the Buddhist precepts ever since her childhood. She was determined to help end the suffering this world. Thus, she had no intentions of getting married. Lyu Dungbin's visit was of course uninvited, but he was not afraid of rejection. Instead, he sat in Lady Guanyin's house and refused to leave!

有一天，呂洞賓帶著禮物去探望觀音娘娘，並且向她求婚，但是觀音娘娘從小就學佛修行，立志救助苦難的世人，所以根本不打算結婚。呂洞賓這麼冒失的跑來，當然是被拒絕了。可是呂洞賓居然不怕碰釘子，他竟坐在觀音娘娘家裏不肯走呢！

　　觀音娘娘看他不走，就生氣的說道：「聽說你愛喝酒，又喜歡交女朋友，還殺過蛟龍，這些行為，哪裏是仙人該做的！現在居然還想做我丈夫，眞是做夢。」

　　呂洞賓聽了，連忙說道：「你誤會了，我喝酒很有分寸，絕不亂喝，說我喜歡交女朋友，那眞是冤枉，至於我殺蛟龍，那是爲民除害！」

　　可是，不管呂洞賓怎麼解釋，觀音娘娘就是不理他。

When Lady Guanyin saw that he would not leave, she became angry and said, "I've heard that you love to drink and go out with many different female friends, and that you've also killed the flood dragon. Would an immortal do such things? And now, you dare fantasize about becoming my husband. You are definitely dreaming!"

Hearing that, Lyu Dungbin quickly replied, "You have misunderstood me. I am a very moderate drinker. I would never abuse alcohol. As for my dates, they are all really innocent. As for my killing the flood dragon, I did it as a service to the people!"

But no matter how hard Lyu Dungbin tried to explain, Lady Guanyin just did not believe him.

Nevertheless, Lyu Dungbin did not give up. He still paid visits to Lady Guanyin. Since Lady Guanyin could no longer bear Lyu's persistent and bothersome visits, she was forced to escape from her house in order to avoid him.

When Lyu Dungbin discovered that Lady Guanyin had left, right away he, too, left to chase after her.

呂洞賓並不死心，以後還是常常去找觀音娘娘。觀音娘娘被他纏得沒法子，最後只好逃走。

呂洞賓發現了，便在後頭一路追。

觀音娘娘乘著雲兒飛呀飛、飛呀飛，飛過了福建的武夷山，飛過了台灣海峽，最後飛來了台北。觀音娘娘覺得台北這地方，氣候溫和、風景又優美，她喜歡得不想走了。

Lady Guanyin sat on top of a cloud. Flying farther and farther, she passed over Fukien's Mt. Wuyi. She flew over the Taiwan Strait to at last arrive in Taipei. Since Lady Guanyin grew fond of the warm weather and the beautiful scenery in Taipei, she did not want to leave.

But what should she do with Lyu Dungbin following close behind her? Instinctively, Lady Guanyin cast a spell. She used one finger to draw a river behind her, stopping Lyu Dungbin from reaching her. From then on, Lyu Dungbin could bother her no more!

可是呂洞賓又在後面追來，怎麼辦呢？觀音娘娘靈機一動，便施了一道法力，用手指頭在身後劃了一道河，隔開呂洞賓，從此以後，呂洞賓就不能再來糾纏她了！

Children, do you know the river that Lady Guanyin created is today's Dansui River (meaning fresh water river), in Taipei? On one side of the river, Lady Guanyin peacefully rests on the top of Mt. Guanyin, enjoying the scenery of the Dansui River.

On the other side, day and night at the Zenan Temple (meaning directional temple), the passionate Lyu Dungbin is forced to watch Lady Guanyin from afar!

Supposedly, after Lyu Dungbin was spurned, he felt very jealous every time he saw couples in love. Therefore, folklore tells us that those who are in love should not go to the Zenan Temple so as not to provoke the gods to separate them. Is that really true? Believe it or not, it is up to you to decide!

Mt. Guanyin and Dansui River

Zenan Temple

小朋友，你知道嗎？那條河就是今天的淡水河，河的這邊，觀音山上的觀音娘娘，很安詳的躺在山頂，欣賞淡水河的風光，

河的那邊呢——指南宮裏的呂洞賓，只能日日夜夜多情的望著觀音娘娘了！

據說呂洞賓失戀以後，看到別人在戀愛，心裏更不是滋味，所以民間傳說：談戀愛的人，可千萬別上指南宮喔！免得觸怒了神明，會被拆散的。真有這回事嗎？只能說信不信由人了！

From Rice into Flowers
The Shy Rainbow
Chinese Children's Stories
Taiwanese Folklore

Chinese Children's Stories **series** consists of 100 volumes; 20 titles of subjects grouped in 5-book sets.

中國孩子的故事 **100** 冊

第 1 ～ 5 冊　　中國民間故事

第 6 ～ 10 冊　　植物的故事

第 11 ～ 15 冊　　動物的故事

第 16 ～ 20 冊　　中國寓言故事

第 21 ～ 25 冊　　中國成語故事

第 26 ～ 30 冊　　節令的故事

第 31 ～ 35 冊　　食物的故事

第 36 ～ 40 冊　　發明的故事

第 41 ～ 45 冊　　十二生肖的故事

第 46 ～ 50 冊　　中國神仙故事

第 51 ～ 55 冊　　孝順的故事

第 56 ～ 60 冊　　中國奇童故事

第 61 ～ 65 冊　　中國神話故事

第 66 ～ 70 冊　　中國文學故事

第 71 ～ 75 冊　　中國名著故事

第 76 ～ 80 冊　　中國名人故事

第 81 ～ 85 冊　　中國歷史故事

第 86 ～ 90 冊　　中國地名故事

第 91 ～ 95 冊　　臺灣地名故事

第 96 ～ 100 冊　　臺灣民間故事

First edition for the United States
published in 1991 by Wonder Kids Publications
Copyright © Emily Ching and Ko-Shee Ching 1991
Edited by Emily Ching, Ko-Shee Ching, and Dr. Theresa Austin
Chinese version first published 1988 by
Hwa-I Publishing Co.
Taipei, Taiwan, R.O.C.
All rights reserved.
All inquiries should be addressed to:
Wonder Kids Publications
P.O. Box 3485
Cerritos, CA 90703
International Standard Book No. 1-56162-047-5
Library of Congress Catalog Card No. 90-60801
Printed in Taiwan